Joy God's Way

"A Journey of Marriage, Parenthood, and God's Joy"

Blue Kendria

Copyright © 2025 by Blue Kendria Berry

All rights reserved.

No part of this publication may be reproduced in whole or in part, or stored in a retrieval system, or transmitted in any form or by any means, electronic, mechanical, photocopying, recording, or otherwise, without written permission and consent of the publisher, except brief quotes used in reviews.

Scripture quotations are taken from the World English Bible (WEB) and are used by permission (CC0). The World English Bible is in the public domain. For more information, visit https://worldenglish.bible.

This book is a work of fiction. Names, characters, places, and incidents either are products of the author's imagination or are used fictitiously. Any resemblance to actual events or locales or persons living or dead is entirely coincidental.

Joy God's Way - "*A Journey of Marriage, Parenthood, and God's Grace*"

(3rd Book in the God's Way Series)

Printed in the United States of America

First Edition, 2025

PAPERBACK ISBN: 979-8-3493-0525-2

HARDBACK ISBN: 979-8-3493-0527-6

EBOOK ISBN: 979-8-3493-0526-9

Red Pen Edits and Consulting

www.redpeneditsllc.com

Thankful to God for His unfailing love and incredible ability to work through me and the continued faithfulness to complete this series of God's Way. Without Him, this journey would not have been possible.

TABLE OF CONTENTS

CHAPTER 1 1

CHAPTER 2 9

CHAPTER 3 13

CHAPTER 4 17

CHAPTER 5 25

CHAPTER 6 31

CHAPTER 7 35

CHAPTER 8 41

CHAPTER 9 45

CHAPTER 10 51

CHAPTER 11 59

CHAPTER 12 69

CHAPTER 13 73

CHAPTER 14 77

CHAPTER 15 81

ABOUT THE AUTHOR 91

CHAPTER 1

After returning from their unforgettable honeymoon, Love and Troy stepped into their home as husband and wife, a deep sense of peace and gratitude settled over them. The honeymoon had been a dream, a whirlwind of adventure, romance, and unforgettable moments but now, they were stepping into something even greater: the reality of building a life together. Troy carried their luggage inside, setting the bags down before pulling Love into his arms. "Welcome home, Mrs. Hayes," he whispered against her hair.

Love smiled, resting her head against his chest. "It feels so good to be home.

They began to settle into their new home, a charming two-story nestled in a peaceful neighborhood lined with tree-canopied streets and kind-hearted neighbors who waved from their porches. It was the house they had purchased shortly after Troy proposed, as they began dreaming and planning the life they were now stepping into together. From the moment they first laid eyes on it during their house-hunting journey, they both knew—it was the one. The home carried the perfect blend of warmth, character, and timeless elegance. With its classic white picket fence, expansive bay windows, and a wraparound porch made for sipping coffee and sharing morning devotionals, it felt like God had hand picked it just for them.

Troy had made sure it sat on a spacious piece of land, envisioning room to grow—a garden, perhaps children one day, and space for new memories to bloom. The walls held promise, and the atmosphere was heavy with the anticipation of blessings waiting to unfold.

With the help of their families, they moved into their new space over the course of three joyful, exhausting days. Laughter echoed through the halls as boxes were shuffled, memories were shared, and the home began to take shape.

As they brought in the last box, Love paused in the middle of the living room, her eyes sweeping across the space. The cozy hearth with its rustic brick fireplace, the bright and open kitchen where she imagined baking Troy's favorite sweets, and the sun-drenched dining area that would soon host countless meals, gatherings, and celebrations—it all felt perfect. Every nook and cranny carried the potential for love to dwell, for their story to be written with faith and laughter.

And with Love's impeccable eye for décor, their house was quickly transforming into a haven—an extension of who they were together: warm, welcoming, anchored in God, and filled with the beauty of new beginnings.

Rather than combine their old furniture, they decided to start fresh. Troy left his furnishings at his bachelor pad, which they turned into an Airbnb due to its prime location in the heart of downtown near the city's most popular events. Love's former home, a cozy space nestled in a serene suburban area, was listed as a rental—perfect for a growing family.

"We did it," Love whispered, leaning against Troy as they stood in the middle of their new home.

Troy wrapped an arm around her shoulders, pressing a kiss to her forehead. "Yes, we did. And this home is going to be filled with so much love."

They worked together to turn the house into a home. Love carefully selected decor that reflected their shared faith and love for God, like framed scriptures on the walls, soft neutral tones, great smelling candles and accents of cream, tan and deep blue that gave the home an elegant yet welcoming feel. Troy, ever the handyman, put together furniture, hung up photos from their honeymoon such as the Eiffel Tower at sunset, the glowing lights of Dubai, the pristine beaches of the Maldives and he ensured everything was just right for his wife.

They were gracefully navigating the beautiful journey of married life—each day bringing its own joy, discovery, and deeper connection. Their weekdays began with shared devotionals at the kitchen table, a steaming cup of coffee in hand, and hearts aligned in prayer. With Troy gently leading their morning reflections, Love felt a renewed strength in her faith. Though she had always believed in the power of prayer, there was something profoundly anchoring about starting each day together in God's presence.

Afterward, they would leave for work hand in hand, sometimes riding together when their schedules aligned. Their lunch breaks still included meetups at Jazzy's or quick strolls through the park just to squeeze in extra time together. In the evenings, they'd cook side by side, Love stirring a pot on the stove while Troy chopped vegetables or set the table, gospel music playing softly in the background.

Weekends became sacred, a beautiful blend of productivity and rest. Saturdays were often spent building their home, from assembling furniture and hanging new art to picking out plants for the front yard. On Sunday mornings, they'd attend church together and come home to change into comfy clothes, sit on the porch with cool glasses of lemonade in hand, and talk about the sermon or their dreams for the future.

Some nights, when the world outside seemed to quiet down just right, they'd find themselves slow dancing barefoot across the living room floor, surrounded by the soft glow of candles and the sweet hum of worship music filling the room. Their home, filled with laughter, prayer, and tenderness, quickly became more than just a house it became their sanctuary.

Every simple moment whether folding laundry together, binge-watching their favorite shows, or walking hand-in-hand through the park was a thread in the tapestry of their love story, woven with grace, peace, and the constant presence of God.

One evening, during dinner, Love sighed contentedly, leaning back in her chair. "I can't believe we're actually married, living together, doing life side by side. It still feels like a dream."

Troy reached across the table, taking her hand. "That's because God's hand has been in this from the start. We prayed for this, and now we're walking in it, enjoying life together."

Love squeezed his hand, her heart swelling. "I'm just so grateful. For you, for us, for everything we've built together."

Troy grinned, standing and pulling her into his arms. "We've only just begun, baby. Even more great things are to come."

After dinner and cleaning the kitchen they settled on the couch after a long day of work and more unpacking, Love sighed happily. "This house already feels like home."

Troy pulled her closer, looking around the space they were creating together. "Because it's not just a house it's our home. And we'll fill it with love, faith, and so many beautiful memories."

One warm September Saturday morning, the golden sunlight bathed their back porch in a soft, comforting glow. Love and Troy sat together on the wooden swing that he built for them, hands gently intertwined, sipping on their morning coffee. The air was calm, the kind of stillness that made everything feel just right. Birds chirped in the distance, and the scent of dew still clung to the grass. It was the kind of morning they cherished quiet, sacred, and simple.

Troy glanced over at Love, his eyes thoughtful as he studied her face. She was beautiful, but he noticed the subtle signs slightly darker circles under her eyes, the way she leaned back a little more wearily, how she hadn't finished her cup of coffee like she usually did.

"Babe," he said gently, placing his mug down on the small side table. "You've been looking really tired lately. Have you been feeling okay?"

She sighed softly, her gaze lost in the view of their backyard the young garden they planted together, the rocking chair Troy surprised her with, and the wind chimes that sang low tunes when the breeze passed through. It was peaceful. Comforting. Yet inside, her body felt different.

Love looked over at him, surprised by the question. She opened her mouth to respond, but then closed it, realizing she couldn't dismiss how she'd been feeling. For the past week or two, she'd noticed the fatigue the kind that settled into her bones. Mornings had brought queasiness she couldn't explain, and her emotions seemed just a little more intense than usual. She had brushed it off, blaming the transition of married life, the emotional high of honeymoon memories, and even the excitement of decorating their new home.

But now, with Troy's eyes watching her so intently, concern etched across his face, the question echoed louder inside her.

She had been more tired lately. Her energy dipped low in the afternoons, and some mornings greeted her with a strange queasiness she couldn't quite explain. Her emotions, usually steady, had felt more fragile. She found herself crying during worship songs that never moved her before, and craving naps in the middle of the day.

She sipped her coffee finally, but the taste was off, kind of bitter, almost metallic. She quietly set it down.

"I... I have been feeling a little different," she admitted slowly, setting her mug down carefully beside his. "More tired than usual. A little off in the mornings. I thought it was just stress or excitement, maybe I'm low on iron or something." She laughed softly, though her eyes didn't quite match the sound.

Troy sat forward, giving her his full attention. "Different how?" he asked, his voice low and steady.

Beside her, Troy arm resting gently across her shoulders, his thumb moving slowly in a circular motion on her arm. He glanced at her, studying her face. His concern was quiet, unspoken, but present in the way he kept looking at her a little longer than usual, in how he'd been watching to make sure she finished her meals or got enough rest.

He didn't say any more but he didn't have to. Love knew he felt it too, that quiet question stirring between them, hovering like a whisper neither of them dared speak aloud just yet.

Maybe it was nothing. Maybe it was everything.

Love paused, feeling her heart begin to race. She looked out across the yard again, her eyes tracing the edges of the fence, the gentle movement of leaves swaying in the breeze.

"I don't know…" she said, almost to herself. "I mean, just different, not really sure how to explain it….." Her voice trailed off as she turned to look at him. Her heart skipped a beat.

The words hung in the air between them, delicate and powerful.

Troy's eyes widened slightly, not with fear, but with concern. He stood slowly, then reached for her hand and gently pulled her to her feet.

"Let's not guess," he said softly. "Call your doctor on Monday. But whatever it is, babe, we'll face it together. Okay?"

Love nodded, her eyes beginning to mist. The realization wasn't fearsome—it was tender, sacred. What if she was pregnant, it would be another chapter in their already beautiful love story, another blessing from the God they prayed to each morning.

Troy pulled her in tighter, holding her close as the morning sun climbed higher, wrapping them in a warmth that felt like peace and promise.

CHAPTER 2

Sunday passed in a quiet blur for Love. Her thoughts swirled with questions she couldn't quite name, emotions she couldn't fully explain. She moved through the day, present but distracted, her heart heavy with the unknown.

She and Troy attended their usual morning church service, slipping into their favorite pew near the front. The worship was powerful, but even the music seemed to echo the uncertainty in her spirit. When the altar call was made, they glanced at each other and instinctively stood. Hand in hand, they walked to the front, their steps slow but full of faith.

As the pastor anointed their heads and prayed, Love bowed her head, silently crying out to God for clarity, strength, and peace. She didn't have all the answers, but she trusted that He did. With her husband's hand wrapped tightly around hers and the warmth of the congregation surrounding them, she found comfort in knowing they were not walking this season alone. Whatever was unfolding, God was already in it and that truth gave her just enough peace to breathe again.

Sunday was unusually quiet in the Hayes household. After returning from church, Love and Troy changed out of their dress clothes and slipped into something more comfortable: Love in an oversized T-shirt and soft leggings, Troy in a pair of joggers and a t-shirt. The energy in the house was peaceful, but a stillness lingered between them, a silence filled not with tension but with unspoken thoughts.

They didn't speak much about the altar prayer, even though both of them had felt something shift while standing side by side at the front of the church. Love busied herself making a light lunch grilled chicken salad sandwiches and sliced fruit while Troy flipped through the television channels but didn't settle on anything to watch. When they sat down to eat, the conversation was minimal, focused mostly on how good the food tasted and how thankful they were for a calm day at home.

After lunch, they migrated to the back porch, sitting in the swing together. The warm September breeze brushed against their skin, carrying the scent of freshly cut grass from somewhere down the street. Love leaned her head against Troy's shoulder, and he gently laced his fingers through hers.

"What a week," Troy said softly, not really expecting a reply.

Love nodded slowly, not trusting herself to speak. She wanted to open up to talk about how tired she'd been, the strange way her body had been feeling, the subtle changes she was trying to make sense of but the words felt too fragile to speak aloud. Not yet.

Troy sat in quiet thought, his thumb tracing small circles on the back of her hand. He wasn't sure why Love seemed distant today, but he didn't press. He'd noticed the small changes too the way she had been sleeping longer, the way her appetite shifted, the emotion in her eyes that seemed to surface for no reason at all. Something was different. He just didn't know what.

Later, they curled up on the couch to watch a movie, but neither of them really paid attention to it. Love's head rested on Troy's chest, her thoughts swirling while his heartbeat played like a calming rhythm in her ear. Occasionally, they exchanged soft smiles, light kisses, and quiet

"I love yous," but even those felt heavier than usual, as though they were carrying more than just affection.

As night fell, they prayed together at the foot of their bed, just like they did every night. But this time, their prayers were filled with deeper longing.

"Lord," Troy prayed gently, "thank You for peace in the unknown. We trust You, even when we can't see the whole picture. Guide us. Strengthen us. And help us hear Your voice clearly."

Love's whispered "Amen" followed, and then silence. They climbed into bed, wrapped in each other's arms, holding on to the comfort of closeness. The air between them wasn't heavy with fear, just the weight of change they could both feel coming, even if neither of them had said the words out loud.

Tomorrow might bring answers, but for now, they rested in the quiet grace of simply being together.

CHAPTER 3

Monday morning, Love sat at her desk looking at the clock waiting on 8 a.m. She had just finished her morning devotional, but her heart still carried a sense of restlessness. As the hold music played softly through the phone speaker, she tapped her fingers nervously against the marble counter. She would normally be sipping her morning coffee but she couldn't stomach the smell.

Her clock chimed 8 and she hurriedly picked up the phone and dialed the number to her doctor's office.

"Hello, Dr. Fenner's office. This is Stephanie, how can I help you today?" a friendly voice finally greeted on the other end.

"Hi, this is Love Hayes, previously Wilson," Love said, trying to keep her voice steady. "I was calling to see if there were any openings... soon. I've just been feeling a little off lately, and I'd like to come in for a checkup. Just to be safe."

The woman on the other end paused. "Let me check... actually, we just had a cancellation for this morning. Can you be here in about an hour?"

Love blinked in surprise. "Yes! Yes, I can. Thank you."

As she hung up, she glanced at the clock. The timing was tight. She sent a message to her boss Harold, to let him know she would be leaving for the remainder of the day because she wasn't feeling well. She checked her schedule and thankfully today was clear. She sent messages to Julie and Mark so that they could advise anyone who called for her to leave a message and send her an email. Love grabbed her keys and purse and left the office. Julie saw the message and noticed Love quietly leaving the office. She had noticed something had been off since she returned from their honeymoon but wasn't sure what it was. She prayed that everything was okay for her boss and friend.

As Love slipped into the seat of her SUV, she called Troy.

"Hey my love," he answered quickly, the sounds of movement in the background.

"Hey babe, I just got off the phone with my doctor. They had a cancellation, so I'm headed there now."

"Wait—this morning?" he asked, the concern in his voice wrapping around every word.

"Yeah, I know it's last minute, but I'd rather not wait."

Troy sighed. "I wish I could go with you, but I've got that client meeting I can't reschedule. Can you let me know how it goes as soon as you're done?"

"Of course," she said gently. "Don't worry, I'm sure it's nothing."

"Still... I'm praying, okay?"

"I know," she whispered. "Me too."

She slid her phone into her purse and headed to her doctor's office.

The waiting room smelled faintly of lavender and hand sanitizer. Love sat quietly, fidgeting with the strap of her purse, her heart thudding louder than it should have for a routine appointment.

After a brief wait, she was called back. The nurse asked the usual questions, checked her vitals, and smiled politely before leaving her alone in the softly lit exam room.

Dr. Fenner entered a few minutes later, all warmth and calmness. "Love, it's good to see you. You mentioned not feeling like yourself lately?"

Love nodded. "Yes, just... tired, emotional, a little queasy here and there."

Dr. Fenner smiled knowingly, then asked a few more detailed questions. After a thoughtful pause, she stood. "I'd like to run some tests and get some blood. Just to be thorough."

Love agreed and followed the instructions without much thought, trying not to let her nerves get the best of her.

When the doctor returned, her expression was gentle but purposeful. She sat beside Love, holding a small clipboard in her hand.

"Love," she said softly, "your results came back... and it looks like you have tested positive —"

Her words blurred for a moment as the weight of the news hit Love like a gentle wave— this unexpected news left her in awe.

She blinked. Her mouth parted, but no words came. Her heart was racing.

The room felt still, suspended in a sacred kind of silence. She left the office in a daze, not sure how to feel or what to say. She thought about calling her mom or stopping by but decided against it.

She sat silently as her mind replayed every word the doctor had spoken. It didn't feel real, at least not yet.

As she drove home she was still in a daze the entire trip home. She pulled into a general store along the way. If nothing else, she could lean into the age-old remedy passed down through generations ginger ale and saltine crackers. She slowly pushed the cart down the aisles, tossing in a few other items though she barely registered what she was doing.

Everything felt surreal, as if she were watching someone else go through the motions.

Still on autopilot, she drove from the store to home in silence. She kept the music off, letting the silence wrap around her like a thin veil. She pulled into the driveway and sat in the car for a moment, hands still gripping the wheel. Her eyes drifted to the house—their house—the one they had prayed over, built dreams in, laughed in, worshiped in. Now everything felt like it was shifting under her feet.

She got home pulled into the garage and sat in the car. She couldn't hold the tears any longer, she quietly sobbed as she thought of how to tell Troy.

Once inside, she put the bags onto the kitchen counter and slowly made her way to the living room. She sank into the couch, curling her legs beneath her, the stillness of the room pressing in around her. For a few moments, she just sat there, blinking back the sting in her eyes, her fingers nervously tracing the fabric of the throw pillow beside her.

And then, again the tears came.

Soft at first—gentle, uncertain—but then deeper. She buried her face in her hands and quietly sobbed yet again, letting the emotions pour out freely now that she was alone.

She wiped her face and let out a long, trembling breath. One thing she did know: God was with her. Just like He had been through every chapter of her story. She just needed a little more courage to begin this next one.

And she needed Troy.

CHAPTER 4

Love remained on the couch for what felt like hours, the soft ticking of the wall clock the only sound breaking the silence of the room. Her eyes, now puffy from crying, stared at nothing in particular just the quiet space in front of her, as her mind raced with a thousand thoughts.

She had rehearsed what she might say to Troy at least a dozen times, and yet every version felt either too much or not enough. The words just wouldn't come. Nothing could quite capture what she was feeling the weight of it, the uncertainty wrapped up in this unexpected news.

Finally, with trembling fingers, she picked up her phone. She knew today was full for him back-to-back meetings and project deadlines, so calling him felt like the wrong move. She opened their message thread, the one filled with sweet check-ins, playful banter, and scripture verses they shared with each other throughout the day.

Her thumbs hovered over the keyboard before she finally typed:

"Hey babe, I'm home from the doctor's office. I'll explain everything when you get home, I love you."

She hit send, then held the phone close to her chest, as if the nearness of it would somehow bring her closer to him in that moment.

A few minutes later, his response came through:

"Okay."

Just one word. Short and simple. But she knew Troy. That "okay" meant he heard her but was uncertain.

She placed the phone beside her, pulled the throw blanket over her lap, and exhaled deeply. The hardest part wasn't sending the message—it was waiting for the moment when she would look into his eyes and say the words that would change their lives forever.

Troy paced the corner of the conference room as the meeting wrapped up. His mind had been half in, half out the entire time. He tried to focus, tried to listen as his team updated him and their client on progress reports and timelines, but all he could hear—over and over—was the sound of Love's voice from earlier that morning.

~I was able to get a last-minute appointment... I'm heading to the doctor now~

It had caught him off guard. He just knew, somehow, that the appointment would be scheduled on a day when he could be by her side. That's how things always seemed to work for them—divinely aligned. But not today. Today, he had meetings he couldn't move and a schedule he couldn't escape.

As he walked back to his office, his heart beat heavily in his chest. He didn't want to be anxious. He didn't want to be afraid. But as much as he trusted God, as much as he leaned into his faith, he was also human. And right now, fear had crept into the quiet spaces of his mind.

He closed the door behind him and sank into his chair, letting out a long, shaky breath. When he finally looked down at his phone, a message from Love was waiting for him:

"Hey babe, I'm home from the doctor's office. I'll explain everything when you get home, I love you."

He stared at the screen for a long moment before replying with the only word he could muster:

"Okay."

But it wasn't okay. Not really. He wanted to be strong. He needed to be strong for her. Yet the uncertainty of it all had his chest tightening, his thoughts spiraling into every worst-case scenario.

What if it was serious?

What if something was wrong?

What if... what if God was preparing him for something he wasn't ready to face?

Troy lowered his head into his hands, and the tears he'd been holding back began to fall. Not loudly. Not dramatically. Just a quiet release of everything he'd been trying to keep contained.

"God... please," he whispered into the stillness of the room. "Please don't take her from me."

He wept into his palms, shoulders shaking with silent sobs, letting out the fear he couldn't say out loud. He wasn't supposed to break—not like this. He was the one who prayed over her every morning, the one who kept their hearts anchored in God's word, the one who had promised to be her rock.

But right now, he wasn't the rock he was the one crumbling. And yet, even in his brokenness, he still believed. He still hoped.

"Lord," he said through clenched teeth, "you gave me this promise, this woman. You said she was my helpmate, my blessing. This can't be over so soon. I trust You. I do... but I'm begging You... let this be something we can face together. Please let her be okay."

He wiped his face, stood to his feet, and breathed in deeply. This was the only moment he would allow himself to fall apart. Because when he walked through that door tonight, he needed to be whole again for her.

No matter what she had to tell him, he would stand firm beside her. Together, they would face it.

There was a knock on Troy's office door, and he quickly wiped the tears from his eyes, trying to compose himself. "Come in," he said, his voice hoarse.

James stepped inside, his eyes scanning the room before landing on Troy. He could tell something wasn't right. "Troy, you okay, man?" he asked, concern lacing his voice. "You didn't seem like yourself during the meeting, and you've been sitting in here for almost an hour."

Troy glanced at the clock, shocked at how much time had passed without him realizing it. He had been so lost in prayer, in his thoughts, and in his emotions that the minutes slipped away unnoticed. "Yeah, I'm…" His voice trailed off, his emotions catching in his throat. He wasn't okay, not at all.

James walked around to the other side of Troy's desk, his hand gently landing on his shoulder. "It's okay, man," he said softly.

Troy swallowed hard and looked up at his friend, his eyes brimming with unshed tears. "No, man… I'm not okay," he confessed, his voice breaking. "We just got married, and now something is going on with Love. I'm scared, man. I don't know what's happening, and I can't be there for her right now. I feel so helpless." His head dropped, his shoulders slumping under the weight of the fear and uncertainty.

James stood quietly for a moment, allowing Troy the space to let the words out. Then, he squeezed Troy's shoulder. "It's going to be okay, Troy," he said gently. "I know when your faith gets weak, it's always good to have friends who can have faith for you."

Troy's eyes filled with more tears, and he nodded, though the uncertainty still clouded his heart. Before he could say anything more, he heard the soft murmur of voices at the door. His team had gathered, standing there with worried looks on their faces. They had been observing his behavior all day, and it was clear something was wrong.

"We can all tell something's going on with you after your wife called," one of them said. "Troy, let us have faith for you and with you."

James smiled warmly, his hand still on Troy's shoulder. "We're a team," he said. "Can we pray for you man?"

Troy looked up at them, his heart heavy but grateful for the support. His voice was barely a whisper. "Yes," he said, tears streaming down his face. "I can use some prayer right now."

Without a moment's hesitation, James stepped forward, and everyone filed into the room, surrounding Troy in a circle. James gently placed his hand on Troy's shoulder, grounding him with his presence. As the team gathered close, James led them in prayer.

"Lord," James began, his voice steady but filled with heartfelt emotion, "we come to You today not knowing what's happening with Love, but we trust in Your sovereignty. We ask for Your peace to surround them both. We ask that You give them strength, clarity, and comfort, knowing that You are the one who sees all and knows all."

The room grew quiet as James spoke, each person in the circle silently agreeing with every word.

"Thank You for this beautiful couple, Lord," James continued. "No matter what, we know You will be there with them every step of the way. You didn't bring them together, to bless them, to love them, to unite them, just to leave them now. You are their strength, and we stand together in faith for them."

He paused, and Troy felt a warmth spread through him, a sense of peace that he had been desperately needing. James's words seemed to settle the turmoil in his chest, if only for a moment.

"And Lord, we want Troy to know," James added, his voice growing softer but more resolute, "that no matter what happens, we've got his back. We're here for him, for Love, and for whatever comes next."

"Amen," everyone said in unison.

Troy slowly raised his head, the weight on his heart beginning to feel a little lighter. "Amen," he whispered, his voice breaking but full of gratitude. He wiped his eyes, a faint smile tugging at his lips. He had been so overwhelmed, so consumed by fear, but in that moment, surrounded by his friends and colleagues, he felt a renewed sense of strength and peace.

He stood up, turning to James. Without a word, he pulled him into a tight hug, both men holding on for a moment longer than usual. "Thank you, man," Troy said, his voice thick with emotion. "Thank you so much."

James smiled and pulled back slightly. "Anytime, Troy. You're not in this alone. We're all here for you."

The others came forward, giving Troy brief but heartfelt hugs, offering their support, and whispering words of encouragement. When the last person filed out, James lingered by the door, his hand resting on the doorknob.

"Go home, man," James said. "We don't have any more meetings today, so I'll handle everything else. You need to be with Love right now."

Troy looked at him, the exhaustion in his eyes, but a sense of peace starting to return. "Thanks, James," he said softly. "I think I will take you up on that offer."

He grabbed his keys and wallet, giving one last glance around the office before heading out. He stopped at the door, turning to thank everyone once more. "Thanks again, all of you," he said. "I don't know what I'd do without this team."

As he walked through the office, his thoughts were focused entirely on Love. Whatever they were facing, whatever the results of her doctor's visit would be, he knew one thing for sure he wasn't facing it alone.

And neither was she.

He drove home in silence ready for whatever was next.

Love was pacing the floor not sure how to tell Troy the news but ready to get to it.

CHAPTER 5

Love had spent hours putting things together, her heart racing as she put the final touches on things for when Troy arrived home. She knew this was something they would both remember forever. She knew they both had been so worried today, consumed with their thoughts about her doctor's appointment, but she was determined to change the mood and bring back the joy into their lives. She just hoped she could pull it off without crying.

She had spent hours preparing everything—the notes, the hidden messages, and the little details that would guide Troy through this. She knew how much Troy loved riddles, and this was going to be the perfect way to distract him, to shift his focus from the uncertainty of the past few hours to what was coming.

She carefully placed the first note at the front door, making sure it was just out of view. It was simple, yet perfect. Her handwriting was neat, just as it had been when she'd written their wedding vows. "Follow the path," it read, a playful hint that something awaited him, though he didn't know what.

The next note was tucked under the mug where they always started their mornings, so he would find it as he entered the kitchen. She smiled as she imagined him reading it, and then heading off to the next spot: "To find the next clue, head where we start each day, where we share our quiet moments and love to pray." She knew he'd love this part, especially because their morning devotionals were so sacred to them.

Moving quickly, Love placed the third note in the bedroom, under the pillow, where Troy would undoubtedly be lying down later, wondering what was going on. "You're getting closer," the note read. "But only halfway there, now look for the place we show we care. She chuckled to herself, knowing their bedroom was more than just a place for rest—it was where they shared everything, the highs and lows of their daily life together.

She stepped back and surveyed the scene—her heart pounding, her nerves tingling. Troy had no idea what was coming and honestly neither did she. This wasn't just about telling him something important, it was life changing. Love wasn't sure how he would react to the final results, but she knew together they would make it.

She took a deep breath, hoping she'd managed to hold it together. When she looked at the living room, she saw the last clue resting on the couch—her final masterpiece. "Now, my love, I want you to know, it's time for the final clue to show. You've journeyed far, but the treasure is near, so sit down where we dream of our future, my dear."

The words would pull him closer to the moment she knew would change everything.

Her heart fluttered with anticipation as she heard the sound of Troy's car pulling into the driveway. He was home. She quickly checked her watch—he was early but on time.

Love felt a wave of nervous excitement wash over her. As he entered the house, she remained quiet, her heart racing. She watched him pause at the first note, a slow smile spreading across his face as he read it. Then, with a deep breath, he began to follow the path she had laid out for him, completely unaware of what was about to happen.

This was it.

When Troy finally arrived home that afternoon, his heart was still heavy, but he felt a flicker of hope after the prayer and support from his friends. He couldn't wait to get home to Love, to hold her, and hear what she had to say about the doctor's appointment.

As he opened the door, he was immediately greeted by an unfamiliar sight. The lights in the house were dimmed, and there was a soft, cozy glow that made the place feel warm and intimate. He stepped inside, taking a deep breath, and paused when he saw a small note on the floor, next to the entryway.

"Follow the path."

Troy smiled, knowing immediately that Love had something planned, even though he wasn't sure what. He bent down to pick up the note and followed the instruction, intrigued. The living room, usually simple and cozy, was now scattered with little clues—pieces of paper with mysterious riddles written on them.

With a mix of curiosity and excitement, he picked up the first riddle.

"To find the next clue, head where we start each day, where we share our quiet moments and love to pray."

Troy chuckled softly, recognizing it immediately. He headed to the kitchen, where they often started their mornings with a cup of coffee and shared devotions. He found another note under his favorite mug.

"You're getting closer, but only halfway there, now look for the place where we show how much we care."

His heart warmed at the thought of their shared affection and care for each other. Without wasting a second, he walked down the hallway to their bedroom, where Love had placed the next clue on their bed.

"A home of laughter, joy, and love, where we talk, laugh, and sometimes argue—now go where we relax and rise above."

Troy knew she was sending him on a little scavenger hunt, probably as a way to ease his nerves, and he appreciated the effort. He walked into the living room, his eyes scanning the room until he found the final clue tucked inside the pages of their favorite book, the one they often read together before bed. He smiled, loving how well she knew him.

"Now, my love, I want you to know, it's time for the final clue to show. You've journeyed far, but the treasure is near, so sit down where we dream of our future, my dear."

His heart raced as he realized what was happening. His palms grew slightly sweaty as he walked to the couch, where he and Love spent so many evenings, wrapped up in each other's arms. Sitting down, he picked up the last note, which was slightly different from the others. It felt heavier—like it held a secret, a big one.

"The best adventure, Troy, is yet to come, and you're going to be a father. We're pregnant, love. Our journey has only just begun."

Troy's hands trembled as he read the words again. His eyes widened as he took in the news, his heart pounding in his chest. Pregnant? They were going to have a baby? It didn't quite feel real, and yet, there it was right in front of him, in the form of Love's perfect handwriting.

He sat in silence for a moment, the words sinking in, and then the overwhelming wave of joy and disbelief hit him all at once. He couldn't believe it. He was going to be a father. The thought both excited and terrified him, but more than anything, he was filled with an overwhelming sense of love and gratitude. His eyes filled with tears, and he sat back, holding the note to his chest.

Love had been silently moving through the house inconspicuously with him. As he opened the last note Love appeared at the doorway, her soft footsteps nearing him. When she saw his face, the smile tugging at the corners of his lips, she knew instantly that he had read the last clue.

"I wanted to tell you in a special way," she said, her voice soft but laced with excitement. "I thought you'd like to figure it out. I wanted to make it a moment we'd always remember."

Troy stood up, still holding the note in his hand. He couldn't find the right words at first he was too overwhelmed with emotion. Then, he looked at her, tears brimming in his eyes, and pulled her into his arms.

"You're pregnant?" he whispered, as if he couldn't quite believe it. "We're having a baby?" "Is this why you have been feeling tired and that unexplainable feeling?"

Love nodded, her eyes shining with joy. "Yes, that is why I have been so tired and yes, we are, Troy. You're going to be a dad. I'm so scared, but I know we'll be okay because we have each other."

Troy's hands gently cupped her face, and he kissed her deeply, pouring every ounce of his love and happiness into that kiss. When they pulled away, he couldn't stop smiling.

"I'm going to be a dad," he repeated, a quiet laugh escaping him. "I'm so proud of you. I'm proud of us."

Love looked up at him, her heart full. "We're in this together," she whispered, her hand resting on his chest, over his rapidly beating heart. "I love you so much."

"I love you more," Troy responded, his voice thick with emotion. "And I can't wait to start this new chapter of our lives with you. We're going to be amazing parents."

The weight of their new journey was just beginning to settle in, but in that moment, surrounded by the clues, the surprises, and the love they had built, they knew they were ready for whatever came next. Together, they kneel and pray, thanking God for this incredible blessing.

CHAPTER 6

It had been a challenging couple of months for Love. The constant nausea, frequent trips to the bathroom, and overwhelming fatigue were starting to take their toll on her. By the time she hit two months into her pregnancy, it became impossible to continue hiding what was going on. At work, people were starting to notice her pale complexion and frequent breaks. Love had tried her best to keep up appearances, but she couldn't ignore how much harder it was getting to keep things under wraps. It was time to confide in someone, and there was no one she trusted more than Julie.

Julie had been her executive assistant and friend for years, and Love knew she could count on her to keep the secret safe until they were ready to announce the pregnancy. So, on a beautiful Friday morning, sitting in her office feeling very nauseous, Love decided to take the plunge.

"Julie, she called on the phone, can you come in here please," Love said, her voice low, a mixture of excitement and nervousness dancing in her chest.

Julie raised an eyebrow, immediately sensing that something important was coming. She got up and walked into Love's office, closing the door behind her and sitting in a chair facing Love.

"I need to tell you something." Love hesitated for a moment, "I'm pregnant," she whispered, her voice barely above a murmur.

Julie's eyes widened in shock, and then her face broke into a bright, joyful smile. "Oh my gosh! Mrs. Hayes, I'm so happy for you!" she exclaimed, unable to hold back her excitement.

Love's smile widened, the weight of her secret now lifting just a little. "Thank you, Julie. It feels so good to finally tell someone. I've been so tired, and I am trying to keep up the act but it is getting hard."

Julie nodded understandingly. "I can only imagine. I noticed you've been running to the bathroom a lot lately. I thought maybe you were just coming down with something, but I didn't want to ask."

Love chuckled softly, feeling a wave of relief that Julie hadn't pressed her earlier. "Yeah, it's been rough. But, um, we plan on keeping it a secret until after the first three months. Please, just keep it between us."

"Absolutely," Julie said, holding a finger up to her lips in a playful gesture of secrecy. "Mum's the word. I won't say a word to anyone."

"Thank you, Julie," Love said, feeling a surge of gratitude toward her friend. "I really appreciate it. And I may need a little help here and there just keeping things quiet."

"No problem at all," Julie replied, her tone warm and reassuring. "You let me know if you need anything, okay?"

As Julie turned to head for the door, Love called out to her, a playful smile tugging at the corners of her lips. "Actually, there is one thing I could use..."

Julie paused and turned back. "What's that?"

"Ice," Love said with a laugh. "I need plenty of ice. It's the only thing that keeps the queasiness at bay."

Julie laughed and nodded. "I got you, boss. I'll be back in a minute."

Not long after, Julie returned with a big cup of ice, the little cubes filling the large styrofoam cup. She'd tucked the cup carefully into a company bag so that no one would notice. When she handed it to

Love, they shared a giggle. It felt so good to be able to finally be open with someone.

Love peeked inside the bag, grinning when she saw the ice cubes gleaming back at her. "You're a lifesaver, Julie. This is exactly what I needed."

"I've got your back, always," Julie said, smiling brightly. "You let me know if you need anything else, okay? Anything at all."

Love took the bag, feeling a sense of peace settle over her. With Julie now in the know, she could breathe a little easier. She had someone she could trust, and it made carrying this secret just a bit lighter. She thought about how soon they would be able to tell everyone, but for now, she would savor these quiet moments, just her, Troy, and their little secret. The journey ahead was still full of unknowns, but at least now, she wasn't alone in it.

Finally, the day of their first ultrasound arrived. Love couldn't help but feel a sense of nervous excitement. She had seen the sonograms online, and heard stories from friends, but this was different. This was her moment—her and Troy's first glimpse at the life they had created together. When they walked into the doctor's office, Love's heart pounded in her chest as they sat down in the waiting room. Troy took her hand, giving it a reassuring squeeze.

"This is it," Love whispered, her voice trembling slightly.

"I know, babe," Troy replied softly, his eyes full of love. "It's going to be amazing."

The ultrasound tech called them in, and as they settled onto the examination table, Love couldn't stop the tears from welling up in her eyes. When the technician placed the cold gel on her belly and began moving the wand, it only took a few moments before the sound of a tiny heartbeat filled the room. Love's breath caught in her throat, and she gripped Troy's hand so tightly she was almost afraid she would hurt him.

"I can hear it," she whispered, tears streaming down her cheeks. "I can hear our baby's heartbeat."

Troy's eyes welled up with tears as well, overwhelmed with emotion. "We're really going to be parents," he said, his voice thick with wonder.

Love nodded, unable to speak as the reality of the moment sank in. The doctor continued the scan, and Love and Troy exchanged glances, both of them trying to process the fact that this tiny little heartbeat was the beginning of their family. The whole experience made everything feel so much more real. The life they had prayed for, the life they had dreamed about, was on its way.

As they left the doctor's office, they both fell into a peaceful silence, holding hands, each lost in their thoughts. They decided to keep the pregnancy a secret for a while longer, treasuring these early moments between just the two of them. There was something sacred about it, the quiet anticipation of a future that was still unfolding. The love they shared and the life they were creating felt like a beautiful secret, one that only they knew about at least for now. They knew that soon enough, the whole world would be celebrating with them. But for today, they held on to the precious moments between them, knowing that this was just the beginning of a beautiful journey.

CHAPTER 7

One Saturday in late October, as the crisp air of autumn settled in and the days grew shorter, Love and Troy hit the end of their first trimester. With hearts full of joy and excitement, they decided it was finally time to share their big news with their family and friends. They had been waiting patiently for this moment, agreeing early on to keep the pregnancy a secret until the end of the first three months. It hadn't been easy to keep this beautiful secret to themselves, especially with all the emotions swirling within them, but they were determined to follow the advice of their doctor and cherish these early days just the two of them.

Now, with the first trimester behind them and their hearts brimming with love, they set out to make this announcement special. Their house was filled with laughter and warmth as they prepared for a reveal cookout, a gathering they had planned for weeks. Both Love and Troy had always enjoyed hosting gatherings, but this one was different. It wasn't just about burgers on the grill and cold drinks; it was about celebrating the life they were creating together, surrounded by the people who meant the most to them.

Love was a flurry of energy, despite the morning sickness and fatigue that had become a part of her daily routine. The nausea that had accompanied her mornings for weeks still lingered, but she powered through, knowing that today was a day of celebration. As she chopped vegetables for the salad, she caught Troy watching her from the doorway, his eyes soft with affection. He had been so supportive through all the ups and downs of her first trimester. Every morning, he would bring her ice, ginger tea to settle her stomach, rub her back when the nausea was unbearable, and even hold her close when she needed comfort after a long, tiring day. Troy had been a rock, a constant source of love and reassurance, and she couldn't wait to share the joy they'd both been carrying in their hearts.

As the guests began to arrive, Love and Troy shared knowing glances, their hands brushing together as they welcomed family and friends into their home. The moment they'd been waiting for had finally arrived. They'd decided to reveal their news with a small twist, keeping it fun and lighthearted. After the meal, once everyone was settled in and the sun began to set, they gathered everyone around the fire pit in the backyard. The warm light of the flames flickered against their faces as they held hands and looked out at the people they loved most.

Troy smiled at Love, and she returned the smile, her eyes twinkling with excitement. "We want to thank everyone for coming. We have some gifts for everyone. They handed out gifts from the cart that they rolled out with them. Wait before you open please. So we've got a little surprise to share with you all tonight," he said, his voice full of joy. "We've been keeping this a secret for a while, but now that we're in the clear, we're ready to tell you. So, if everyone can open your gift, Love and I want to share something very special."

As everyone eagerly unwrapped their gifts, the area filled with gasps and joyful laughter. Inside each box was a small plush stork holding a scroll in its beak, and when unrolled, the scroll read in elegant gold script: **"Baby Hayes arriving April 12th."**

The parents of Love and Troy blinked in surprise before noticing the soft t-shirts nestled beneath the stork. Love's mom and Troy's mom held up theirs with tears welling in their eyes **"I'm going to be** a Grandma" was printed in bold, playful lettering. The dads held up their shirts proudly, grinning as they read **"Promoted to Grandpa."**

Meanwhile, the siblings erupted in cheerful shouts, holding up their shirts that read **"Auntie in Training"** and **"Cool Uncle Loading..."** Love stepped forward as everyone was opening their gifts, holding her breath for just a moment before speaking. " Yes, we're going to be parents," she said, her voice filled with emotion.

The backyard was soon filled with hugs, happy tears, and joyful chatter and plenty of congratulations flying their way. The surprise was everything Love and Troy hoped for intimate, meaningful, and unforgettable. This wasn't just a cookout anymore; it had become the celebration of a growing family and the beginning of a brand-new chapter in their lives.

Their families and friends gathered around them, hugging them tightly and congratulating them on their growing family. It felt like the weight of the world had been lifted off their shoulders, and Love couldn't help but smile as Troy pulled her close, kissing the top of her head.

"Thank you and please keep us in your prayers," Love said, her voice trembling slightly. "We're so excited for this next chapter in our lives."

As the afternoon wore on, the golden sunlight filtered through the trees, casting a soft, warm glow over the backyard. Laughter danced through the air, mixing with the aroma of grilled food and the joyful chatter of family and friends. Love leaned against Troy as they sat side by side, taking in the scene—nephews running through the grass, parents wiping away happy tears, siblings still grinning from the surprise.

They shared stories, reliving moments from their journey—how they met, how Troy proposed, and now, the news that had brought everyone together. Every hug, every word of encouragement felt like another layer of love wrapped around them. The cookout, which had started as a simple family gathering, had become a memory etched in joy and hope—a celebration of new beginnings, not just for their baby, but for their growing family.

As the sun dipped low, casting a soft orange hue across the sky, the guests began to leave, still buzzing with excitement. Love and Troy stood by the gate, waving and exchanging lingering goodbyes, holding hands tightly, hearts full.

Later that evening, the house was quiet again. Dishes were washed, leftovers stored, decorations still fluttering in the breeze outside. Love lit a candle in the living room while Troy turned on soft music. They curled up on the couch together, Love resting her head on Troy's chest as his hand gently stroked her belly.

"I still can't believe everyone knows now," she whispered, smiling softly.

Troy kissed her forehead. "We're really doing this, babe. You and me… we're going to be parents."

She looked up at him, eyes glistening. "You're going to be such an amazing dad."

"And you," he said, brushing a strand of hair from her cheek, "are already an amazing mom."

Their lips met in a tender kiss, one filled with gratitude, hope, and promise. Slowly, they moved from the couch to their bedroom, drawn to one another by the deep love that had carried them through every chapter so far.

As the night settled in around them, their home quiet and peaceful, they made love wrapped in the intimacy of shared dreams and whispered prayers. It was a sacred moment between two souls knit together by faith, now intertwined in the miracle of life. The night ended in each other's arms, the soft rhythm of their breathing matching the steady beat of the new life growing inside Love a beautiful, quiet promise of what was to come.

CHAPTER 8

Even with the excitement of the announcement, the reality of the pregnancy began to set in. Troy was there for her every step of the way, his unwavering support a constant comfort. He made sure to keep the house stocked with ginger tea, saltine crackers, and anything else he thought might help her feel better. When she wasn't feeling well, he would sit beside her, rubbing her back and whispering words of encouragement until the sickness passed. Even through the hardest days, Love knew she wasn't alone.

As the weeks passed, Love's body began to change in ways she hadn't fully anticipated. She had read the books, followed the apps, and heard stories from other moms, but nothing quite prepared her for the full experience of pregnancy, the beautiful, emotional, and sometimes exhausting transformation happening from the inside out.

Her once-fitted clothes began to feel snug, and her favorite jeans no longer buttoned comfortably. She laughed the first time Troy saw her struggling to pull them on and immediately offered to go shopping for maternity leggings that same day. "Babe, your comfort is priority number one," he said, grinning as he held up stretchy pants like they were a sacred gift. They both laughed, but there was something special about the way he cared for her, it made her feel seen, cherished, and safe.

Yet, it wasn't just the physical changes that took Love by surprise, it was the emotional rollercoaster that caught her most off guard. One moment she'd be glowing with joy, hand on her belly, dreaming about baby names and nursery colors. The next, she'd be crying into a pillow because a commercial on TV showed a puppy being adopted. Small things became monumental, and the emotional weight of carrying life inside her often left her feeling vulnerable.

There were days when she'd stand in front of the mirror, touching her growing belly with both wonder and uncertainty. Was she ready for this? Would she be a good mom? Was the baby okay? Sometimes the fear whispered louder than her faith, and it took every ounce of strength to silence the doubts.

But through every hormonal swing, every late-night craving, and every tearful moment Troy remained her anchor. His love was consistent, unwavering. When she was too tired to cook, he whipped up her favorite meals. When she woke up in the middle of the night restless and uncomfortable, he would rub her back until she drifted off again. He never made her feel like a burden. In fact, he reminded her often, "You're doing something extraordinary, Love. I'm proud of you."

He prayed over her belly every night before bed, his hands gently resting on her stomach. "God, thank you for this gift," he'd whisper, his voice steady and sincere. "Protect our baby and give Love peace and strength. We trust You, Lord."

Those prayers became a lifeline, grounding her, centering her, reminding her of the bigger picture. This wasn't just about the changes or the discomfort, this was about the miracle growing inside her, the child God had entrusted them to raise in love and faith.

And in the quiet moments, when the world felt too heavy, Love would lean into Troy's chest, his arms wrapped around her like a shield. He was her calm in the chaos, her balance when everything felt out of control.

Though her emotions swung wildly and her body transformed more each day, one thing remained certain she didn't have to go through this journey alone. With Troy by her side, she felt held. Supported. Loved. And more than anything, she knew they would face each new week of this journey together hand in hand, heart to heart, with faith lighting the way.

CHAPTER 9

As Love eased into her second trimester, something beautiful began to shift. The constant nausea that had once shadowed her mornings finally began to fade, and the heavy fatigue that had weighed her down started to lift. Her energy returned slowly at first—little bursts of motivation and lightness but soon enough, she was smiling more, humming to herself again, and moving with a new kind of joy. Though she still had her moments, she was beginning to feel more like herself again—stronger, lighter in spirit, and ready to fully embrace this season.

She was starting to *feel* like herself again, only now with a baby growing inside of her a glowing, sacred reminder of the life she and Troy were building together.

One quiet evening in early November, Love was curled up on the couch in her favorite knit blanket, the soft glow of the Christmas lights flickering across the walls. A gentle flurry had just started falling outside, and the house was peaceful, wrapped in the stillness of winter. Troy had just returned from work, loosening his tie and sitting beside her, his hand naturally resting on her knee.

They were halfway through a Christmas movie, the kind they both loved warm, simple, full of holiday cheer. Love had just taken a sip of peppermint tea when she suddenly froze.

Her eyes widened. She slowly lowered the mug and placed a hand on her belly.

Troy noticed the change in her expression. "You okay?" he asked, concern instantly etching his face.

She didn't speak right away. Instead, her mouth parted into a small, breathless smile. "Troy... I think... I think the baby just kicked."

He sat up straighter, eyes locked on her. "Are you serious?"

Love nodded, her eyes glistening with tears. "It felt like a flutter at first. But that" She paused, gasping slightly. "That was definitely a kick."

Without hesitation, Troy moved closer and placed his hand gently on her belly, his palm warm and steady. For a moment, there was only silence between them, holding their breath, waiting. Then it happened again.

A soft, distinct kick.

Troy's eyes lit up as if he'd just witnessed a miracle. "Oh my gosh," he whispered, staring at her belly as if it were made of stars. "Our baby kicked. I felt it, Love. I felt our baby."

Love let out a soft laugh that turned into a joyful cry. "Our baby is saying hello, daddy."

Troy leaned down, pressing a kiss against her belly. "Hi, little one," he whispered. "We love you so much already."

He rested his head against her, keeping his hand where he felt the life inside her, now moving and making herself known. It was the smallest of kicks, but to them, it was a declaration, *I'm here. I'm growing. I can't wait to meet you.*

They stayed like that for a long time, not needing words, just the quiet reverence of the moment. Love felt overwhelmed with gratitude, and Troy, usually composed, wiped a tear from his cheek.

"Our baby is really real," he finally said, voice cracking.

"Yes," Love whispered, rubbing his back. "And already got your strength."

Troy looked up at her, full of awe and love. "But has your heart."

"Babe," Love said, her voice soft but a little whiny in the way Troy had come to recognize her *pregnancy craving voice*.

Troy looked up from her belly, smiling. "Yes, my love?"

She gave him the most dramatic puppy-dog eyes she could muster. "Can I get my crave bowl?"

Troy chuckled and stood, already knowing exactly what she meant. "Of course you can, Queen Cravings," he teased.

He walked to the fridge and pulled out the special glass bowl she'd prepped earlier, her current favorite: crisp pickles, juicy mango slices, and plump strawberries. The combination was odd to anyone else, but to Love, it was *perfect*.

As he made his way back to the couch, she perked up, eyes lighting with excitement. He handed her the bowl like he was presenting a royal gift.

"Your majesty," he said with a bow, "one crave bowl, freshly chilled."

Love giggled, taking it from him. "Thank you, kind sir. Can you now sit beside me and rub my feet please?"

Troy laughed as he sat down and reached for her feet. "Yes ma'am. Whatever my wife wants, my wife gets."

She popped a pickle in her mouth and leaned into him, smiling. "You're the best, you know that?"

He kissed her cheek. "I try. Besides, seeing you happy is my favorite thing."

They settled in, the sound of Love crunching on pickles and humming with satisfaction filling the room as Troy gently rubbed her feet. Moments like this simple, sweet, full of love made the journey even more special.

Even her cravings had increased. Love craves everything from pickles and ice cream, mango and oreo smoothies to liver and dumplings. Troy happily indulges her every request. They also start attending birthing classes, where Troy is an attentive and loving partner, making her feel supported every step of the way.

By the time Thanksgiving rolled around, the crisp November air felt invigorating instead of exhausting. Love woke up that morning with a deep sense of gratitude, stretching gently in bed and placing a hand on her belly, whispering, "Happy Thanksgiving, little one." Troy stirred beside her and pulled her in for a soft kiss. "Happy Thanksgiving, Mama," he said with a smile, resting his hand over hers.

Love was determined to contribute to the meal this year. Cooking was something she loved, a way to show care and creativity, and with her energy back, she was eager to get back into the kitchen. She had her heart set on making her famous honey-baked cornbread and a sweet potato pie that her grandmother had passed down to her. But her plans were quickly intercepted by their lovingly overprotective families.

When she brought up her Thanksgiving cooking intentions in the group chat, the immediate response from both sides of the family was a firm and unanimous *no*.

Her mother and mother-n-luv called her just to reinforce the message: "Love, baby, you can make one dish and one dessert. That's it. No bending over the oven, no lifting pans, no running around. You are pregnant, and you are going to rest, you hear me?"

Troy's mom chimed in too. "You can bring the flavor, sweetheart, but you're not doing the labor."

Love laughed but knew deep down that their care came from a place of deep love. So she agreed, cornbread and sweet potato pie it was.

That morning, she tied on her favorite apron and moved with a sense of peace and purpose around the kitchen. Troy sat nearby, keeping an eye on her like a hawk but with a smile that betrayed how proud he was to see her glowing again. Every now and then, he'd sneak over and wrap his arms around her from behind, pressing a kiss to her cheek. "You sure you don't need help?" he teased.

"I'm good, babe," she replied, eyes twinkling. "Let me have this."

The house was filled with the warm, rich aroma of spices and brown sugar, of cornbread baking golden in the oven, and sweet potatoes bubbling on the stove. Christmas music played softly in the background, and snow lightly dusted the windows.

When they arrived at her parents' house that afternoon, Love walked in carrying only her two dishes Troy insisted on handling everything else. As she stepped inside, she was immediately greeted by a chorus of family members rushing to take her coat, pull out a seat for her, and make sure she had a comfy pillow for her back.

"Look at our mama glowing!" her sister called out, and Love couldn't help but laugh.

Throughout the day, she was pampered and doted on. She spent most of her time in a cozy armchair, sipping on apple cider, surrounded by stories, laughter, and the warm chatter of family. Every so often, someone would come by and place a hand on her belly, smiling in wonder. Love watched as Troy floated around the house, checking on her, making sure she had everything she needed, and bonding with their families with ease and joy.

As dinner was served, her cornbread dressing and sweet potato pie were hits as always, but more than that, Love felt *present*. Grateful. A part of something sacred.

That evening, as they drove home under the stars, Love rested her head on Troy's shoulder. "I'm so thankful," she whispered.

He kissed her forehead. "Me too. This was our baby's first Thanksgiving… and you made it beautiful."

She smiled, hand on her belly. "Next year, we'll be bringing a little plus one to the table."

Troy grinned. "Best Thanksgiving guest ever."

With her belly beginning to round out and form the sweet curve of new life, there was no more hiding the pregnancy. Her glow became evident, not just in the soft stretch of her skin, but in her eyes, in the way she smiled more freely, laughed more openly, and carried herself with a quiet, graceful confidence.

Love started documenting the journey, taking weekly bump pictures in the mirror with sticky notes showing how many weeks along she was. Troy, with his usual charm, turned it into a whole event, adding silly props or holding up signs that read things like *"Baby's the size of an avocado!"* or *"Dad is already in love."*

They started creating a scrapbook together, filled with ultrasound photos, notes to the baby, scripture verses that spoke to them, and pictures from their daily lives. It became a sacred ritual on Sunday evenings: music playing in the background, Love curled up on the couch, feet in Troy's lap, as they planned pages and laughed over memories they were already making.

CHAPTER 10

At their 20-week appointment, Love and Troy sat hand-in-hand in the dimly lit ultrasound room, the soft hum of machines and the gentle beeping of monitors surrounding them like a lullaby. Love's gown rustled slightly as she adjusted on the table, heart fluttering with excitement and nervousness. Troy hadn't let go of her hand since they walked through the door.

The technician smiled warmly as she applied the cool gel to Love's belly. "Are you ready to see your little one?"

They both nodded, eyes glued to the screen as the image came into view. This time, the picture was so much clearer than before. Their baby was no longer a little dot or peanut-shaped blob, this tiny human now had form and detail. Little fingers wiggled, legs kicked, and the sweet curve of the spine looked like it had been drawn by the hand of God Himself.

"Oh my goodness," Love whispered, her voice catching as tears filled her eyes. "Look at our baby."

Troy leaned in and pressed a kiss to her forehead, his own eyes glistening. "God is so good, Love. Just look at this miracle. That's our baby right there..."

The technician continued to gently glide the wand across Love's belly, pointing things out with practiced clarity. "Here's the heart, beating nice and strong. And here's the spine... toes... hands... and would you like to know the gender?"

Love and Troy exchanged a glance. They had talked about this moment so many times. Initially, they planned to wait, to keep the surprise for the baby shower. But something shifted in the air, the emotions, the magic of the moment, something told them this was it.

Troy smiled, a little tear slipping down his cheek. "You know what? Let's do it. Let's find out right here, right now."

Love squeezed his hand tightly, her heart racing as she nodded. "Yes. Let's meet our baby."

The technician grinned and moved the wand slightly. "Okay then... Let's see... ah, there we go." She turned the screen slightly toward them and typed in a few things before glancing up with a gentle smile. "Congratulations, you two... it's a boy."

Love gasped, covering her mouth with her free hand as a tear spilled over. "A boy..."

Troy let out a breathy laugh, overcome with emotion. "A son..." he repeated in awe. "We're having a son, Love."

He wrapped his arms around her, burying his face in her hair as they held each other, hearts pounding with joy and gratitude.

"I can't believe it," Love whispered. "A son. Oh, God, thank You."

The technician gave them a few quiet minutes before handing them a strip of printed images from the ultrasound. "Here's your little man's first photo shoot."

Troy squeezed Love's hand as they both stared in awe at the screen. Tears welled up in her eyes as she whispered, *"Look at our baby."*

Troy leaned down and kissed her forehead, his voice thick with emotion. *"God is so good, Love. Just look at this miracle."*

They left the appointment floating on air, staring at the color images like they were holding gold in their hands. That evening, they sat on the couch, wrapped in a blanket, with the sonogram pictures laid out on the coffee table.

Troy smiled down at Love, his voice soft and reverent. "We've got a little king growing in there."

Love nodded, resting her head in his hand. "I can't wait to meet him."

And though they decided to still do a fun gender reveal for their family and friends, this private moment, just the two of them and their baby boy, was more precious than they could have ever imagined.

The morning after their appointment, still glowing from the joy of the day before, Love and Troy sat together on the couch, sipping warm tea as the winter sun streamed through the curtains..

As Love rested her head on Troy's shoulder, she looked up with a spark in her eyes.

"Babe," she said with a soft smile, "I think we should tell everyone."

Troy grinned. "The gender?"

She nodded. "Yes. Let's do something simple and sweet. Maybe a video... just for the family."

"I love it," he said, already getting excited. "Let's make it memorable."

Within the hour, Love was in the kitchen whipping up a small, beautifully frosted cake. The outside was simple, white with soft green leaves and tiny gold edible pearls, but the inside was where the magic waited. Troy set up his phone on a tripod, adjusting the frame to capture the moment just right. They changed into cozy neutral outfits, matching cream sweaters and jeans, making it feel intimate and real.

Once the cake was ready, they stood together, a soft instrumental worship song playing faintly in the background. Love and Troy stood next to each other with the cake on the table. With a slow breath and a shared glance, they picked up the knife together and sliced into the cake.

A burst of bright blue spilled from the center, they smiled at each other and kissed.

"It's a boy," they said in unison.

Troy kissed her temple. "Our baby boy."

The camera faded to a white screen with elegant gold lettering that read:

Baby BOY Hayes Coming April 12th

Introducing Jeremiah Isaiah Hayes

Below the message, a small note appeared in Love's handwriting:

"Named for the prophet who taught us to never be afraid to speak what God says...

And the promise that 'Those who hope in the Lord will renew their strength.'"

— With love, Troy, Love, and Baby Jeremiah

They sent the video to their families through a private group message. Within minutes, their phones lit up with excited messages, emojis, and voice notes filled with squeals, praises, and happy tears.

Both Love and Troy's mother facetimed them almost immediately, barely able to speak through their joyful sobs. Love's siblings sent videos of them jumping and dancing, shouting, "We knew it!" And both grandfathers-to-be proudly declared they were going to teach Jeremiah everything they knew.

Love sat beside Troy, her phone buzzing nonstop, and smiled through happy tears. "This little boy is already so loved," she said softly.

Troy kissed her knuckles and whispered, "And so are you."

They sat in the quiet afterward, holding hands, watching their video one more time with tears in their eyes and gratitude in their hearts. It wasn't just a gender reveal, it was the beginning of a new chapter. One they knew would be filled with faith, purpose, and immeasurable love.

Love's nesting instincts kicked in almost overnight. She started organizing the house with a fervor Troy had never seen before. Closets were cleaned, drawers labeled, and bins stacked in color-coordinated order. She became best friends with online baby boutiques and nursery Pinterest boards.

The Saturday before Christmas, they spent hours at baby stores testing out strollers, comparing cribs, and choosing colors for the nursery. They finally settled on a soft neutral theme, creamy whites, warm browns, and gentle forest greens. It felt peaceful, like a little haven of love and rest, a place where their baby would be rocked to sleep in the arms of prayer and protection.

Once they go home from baby shopping Troy painted the nursery himself, careful with every stroke, while Love sat on a chair in the doorway, giving him tips and snacking on frozen grapes. She teased him about the smudges on his shirt and the streaks of paint on his arm. He grinned, "Hey, this is a labor of love. For you. For our little one."

For the first time in years they actually got snow, real snow on Christmas. The snow had fallen the night before, blanketing the quiet neighborhood in a soft, white glow. Love stood at the large bay window, wrapped in a plush cream robe, hands resting gently on her growing belly as she watched the flakes flutter from the sky. Troy came up behind her, wrapping his arms around her and placing a soft kiss on her cheek.

"Merry Christmas, Mama," he whispered with a grin.

Love leaned back into him and smiled. "Merry Christmas, Daddy."

It was their first Christmas in their new home, and it already felt like something out of a dream. The tree stood tall and proud in the corner of their living room, adorned with gold and deep green ornaments, twinkling lights, and a delicate baby's first Christmas ornament they'd bought the week before. Beneath it, wrapped presents spilled out in every direction, gifts for family, friends, and a surprising number already for Baby Hayes.

By mid-morning, the house was alive with the sound of laughter, gospel Christmas music playing softly in the background, and the smell of cinnamon, cloves, and baked macaroni wafting from the kitchen. Both families had come, Love's and Troy's, and the house was filled with chatter, hugs, and good-natured teasing.

Love's mom was in the kitchen helping to prep the Christmas dinner, though she constantly reminded Love to sit down and keep her feet up. Troy's dad was setting up folding chairs near the fireplace for everyone to gather around once gifts were opened. Cousins, siblings, and nieces and nephews were all over the place, enjoying hot cocoa and cookies while sneaking peeks at the growing stack of gifts under the tree.

As the morning turned into early afternoon, it was time for gifts. Troy handed Love a soft blanket and fluffed the pillows behind her while she settled onto the couch. He sat beside her, holding her hand, as the gift exchange began.

Everyone had brought something for the baby.

There were cozy blankets, soft onesies, tiny socks, handmade booties, and picture books. Love's sister and sisters-in-luv had gifted them a baby Bible, with a soft cover and gold-edged pages. Troy's mom gave them a beautiful hand-stitched quilt with the baby's name embroidered in the corner: *Jeremiah Isaiah Hayes.*

Love was moved to tears several times, overwhelmed by the love their families already had for their unborn son. She felt his soft kicks, almost as if he was excited too, and rested a hand on her belly.

"I think he knows he's surrounded by love," she whispered to Troy.

Troy squeezed her hand and smiled. "He sure is."

Once all the gifts were unwrapped and the living room looked like a sea of ribbons and wrapping paper, everyone gathered for prayer before dinner. Troy stood and led the family in a heartfelt prayer, thanking God for the gift of His Son, for the blessing of family, and for the precious life growing inside of Love.

"Lord," he prayed, "thank You for the joy we feel today. We ask that You continue to cover our family with peace and unity. Thank You for trusting us to raise this child in Your love. May we always remember what this season truly means, Your grace, Your promises, and the miracle of new beginnings."

"Amen," everyone said in unison.

Dinner followed, a joyful feast filled with laughter, shared stories, and second (and third) helpings. That evening, as the last of the family headed out into the snowy night, Love and Troy curled up together in front of the fire. The twinkling tree lights cast a warm glow around them, and the sound of their favorite worship song played softly in the background.

"Best Christmas ever," Love said sleepily, resting her head on Troy's shoulder.

"Absolutelyyyyyy," Troy whispered, placing his hand on her belly. "Next year, our baby boy will be in our arms."

They sat there in peace, heartbeats aligned, the quiet night wrapping around them like a blanket. And in that moment, they knew this would be the first of many Christmases filled with joy, love, and the presence of God in their home.

CHAPTER 11

During these months, they grew even closer. They'd lie in bed at night with Troy talking to the baby, whispering stories, singing lullabies, and placing his head on her belly as if he could hear a response. Love would run her fingers through his hair and smile, feeling like the most loved woman in the world.

Some nights, she'd wake up and feel little flutters, soft, gentle kicks that reminded her their baby was growing stronger. The first time she felt it, she gasped and placed her hand on her belly. "Troy!" she whispered in the middle of the night, nudging him awake. "I think the baby just kicked."

Half-asleep, he sat up and placed his hand over hers. They stayed still in the dark, hearts full and breath held, until they both felt it—*a tiny, miraculous movement beneath her skin.*

Troy's face broke into the biggest smile. "That's our baby," he whispered in awe.

However, these months were not without their challenges, Love had backaches, restless nights, and moments of doubt, but they were deeply marked by a sense of joy and anticipation. The baby was no longer just an idea, a dream, they were *real*, and their presence was already shaping their home and hearts.

Together, Love and Troy pressed forward, growing not just as future parents, but as partners. Every heartbeat they heard, every flutter they felt, every decision they made as a couple, brought them one step closer to the day they'd finally hold their little miracle in their arms.

One chilly evening in early February, as the sun dipped behind the trees and the sky blushed with the last light of day, Love stood in the kitchen humming softly, preparing a light dinner. She had insisted she felt good that day, her energy was higher than usual, and she wanted to do something sweet for Troy after he'd been so attentive and protective lately.

But suddenly, a sharp, stabbing pain gripped her lower abdomen. She gasped and grabbed the edge of the counter, her body curling inward instinctively. The pain was unlike anything she had felt so far in her pregnancy. A wave of dizziness followed, blurring her vision and leaving her breathless. She tried calling for Troy, but her voice came out as a soft, strained whisper.

Troy, who had just stepped into the living room to grab a glass of water, heard a thud and rushed back into the kitchen.

"Love!" he shouted, rushing to her side as he found her slumped on the floor, clutching her belly. Panic surged through his chest. "Babe, talk to me, what's wrong?"

She winced, her eyes squeezed shut. "Cramping... it hurts... I don't feel right..."

Without a second thought, Troy scooped her up in his arms and carried her to the car. His heart pounded as he drove to the hospital, the longest fifteen minutes of his life. His hands gripped the steering wheel tightly, and he whispered prayers over and over again.

"God, please... please protect her. Protect our baby. I trust You. I trust You."

Love sat quietly in the passenger seat, breathing slowly, tears falling silently down her cheeks as she prayed in her own heart. "Lord, please... not now. Not this baby. I need this baby. Please cover us."

At the hospital, nurses quickly wheeled her into a room and hooked her up to monitors while Troy sat beside her, clutching her hand tightly, his eyes never leaving her face.

After what felt like hours but was only a little while, the doctor finally came in with a reassuring smile. "The baby's heartbeat is strong, and everything looks stable," he said. "What you experienced was a combination of round ligament pain and possibly a sudden drop in blood pressure. It can happen, especially during the second and third trimester. But," he added gently, "you must take it easy, Love. No lifting, no standing too long, and no overdoing it. Your body's asking you to slow down."

Relief washed over them both, but it was mixed with sobering reality. The moment had shaken them deeply, reminding them just how fragile and precious this journey truly was.

Later that night, back at home, Troy made Love comfortable on the couch, surrounded her with pillows and brought her warm tea and a blanket. He sat at her feet, resting his forehead against her knees.

"I thought I was going to lose you," he said quietly, voice thick with emotion. "Or our baby. I've never felt that kind of fear before."

Love reached for his hand, threading her fingers through his. "I was scared too. But we're okay. He's okay."

They sat in silence for a long moment before Troy spoke again. "No more pushing yourself. Promise me you'll let me help more, even with the little things."

She nodded slowly. "I promise."

Troy reached for his Bible on the end table and opened to Psalms, reading aloud with a steady, prayerful tone. Afterward, they bowed their heads and prayed together—longer than usual, softer than usual, but deeper than ever before.

"God, thank You for covering our baby. Thank You for keeping Love safe. We know You hold our future in Your hands, and we trust You with everything. Give us peace in the unknown, strength when we're weak, and joy even in the hard moments. We're Yours. This baby is Yours."

As they whispered their final "Amen," Troy leaned over and kissed her belly gently.

"Rest now, baby boy," he murmured. "Daddy's got you. And more importantly, God's got you."

Love closed her eyes, breathing in the peace of that moment. The fear had come, but so had grace. And that night, wrapped in each other's love and God's faithfulness, they rested.

Just a few days after the hospital scare, Love had a follow-up appointment scheduled with her OB. The doctor had reassured her before they left the hospital that everything looked okay, but she wanted to do another ultrasound just to be safe and monitor the baby's development more closely.

Troy refused to let her go alone this time. He took the entire day off, holding her hand tightly from the moment they walked into the building until they were back in the exam room. His protective nature had increased tenfold since the scare, and Love didn't mind, his presence was a comfort.

The doctor came in with a warm smile and dimmed the lights. "Let's take a look at your sweet little one, shall we?" she said, squeezing gel onto Love's belly and placing the wand down gently.

Almost instantly, the room was filled with the beautiful, steady rhythm of their baby's heartbeat.

"There it is," the doctor said cheerfully.

Troy let out a small sigh of relief, kissing the back of Love's hand. "That sound never gets old," he whispered.

But then the doctor paused. Her eyes narrowed slightly as she moved the wand to another spot, a subtle look of curiosity crossing her face.

"Hm," she murmured.

Troy's body tensed. "Is something wrong?"

The doctor's lips parted into a soft, surprised smile. "Not wrong... just unexpected." She glanced at the monitor again, then looked at them both. "I'm hearing a second heartbeat."

Love's eyes widened. "A second what?"

The doctor moved the wand again, and sure enough, another tiny but distinct heartbeat echoed through the room.

"There's another baby in there," she said gently, turning the screen so they could both see. "You're having twins."

Troy stood up slowly, leaning closer to the monitor in disbelief. "Are you serious?" he asked, eyes darting between the screen and the doctor.

She nodded, laughing softly. "Very serious. Look—this is Baby A," she pointed, "your little boy. And this," she moved the wand slightly again, "is Baby B... a girl."

Love gasped, her hands flying to her mouth. "A girl?" she whispered, tears instantly welling in her eyes.

Troy sank back into the chair, completely overwhelmed. "Oh my gosh," he breathed. "We're having a boy *and* a girl?"

He turned to Love, eyes wide with wonder, his voice shaking. "Love... twins. We're having twins."

Tears streamed down her face as she reached for his hand. "God is so faithful," she whispered. "We were praying over one miracle and didn't even know He was preparing two."

The doctor smiled, handing them both a few ultrasound images. "They're measuring beautifully. You're halfway there, Mama. But you'll need to rest more from here on out, twins are a little more demanding on the body."

As they left the appointment, Troy couldn't stop smiling, glancing over at Love every few seconds as they walked hand in hand to the car.

"I've gotta start figuring out how to be a girl dad now too," he said, still in awe. "I was just getting used to the idea of diaper duty and matchbox cars."

Love laughed, her heart full. "You're going to be amazing."

That night, they sat together in bed, surrounded by ultrasound pictures. One showed Baby A, their little boy, Jeremiah. The other showed Baby B, their surprise girl, already affectionately being referred to as "Bella."

"We'll call her Isabella Abigail," Love whispered, smiling as she laid the picture against her chest. "Because this was nothing but grace."

Troy nodded, pulling her close. "Jeremiah and Isabella... our double portion."

They prayed again, with fresh tears and new joy, thanking God for not just one promise, but two.

The following weekend, Troy and Love invited both of their families over for a casual dinner. It wasn't unusual for them to host, especially since announcing the pregnancy months ago, but this evening carried a heavier weight for the couple. There had been a scare, a moment where everything felt uncertain, and now, a miracle that needed to be shared.

Love had made her favorite comfort meal: baked ziti, garlic bread, and a big Caesar salad. Troy handled the drinks and set up a cozy dessert table with sweet tea, peach cobbler, and slices of leftover cake from their last date night. Everything looked normal on the outside—but they were both bursting with a mixture of emotions on the inside.

Once everyone had finished eating and were lounging around in the living room, Troy glanced at Love. She gave a small nod, and he stood.

"Can I have everyone's attention for a second?" he said, his voice steady but soft. The room quieted.

"So, this week was a little emotional for us," he began, reaching for Love's hand. She stood beside him. "Love had a pretty rough evening a few days ago. She was having some cramping and dizziness, and I rushed her to the hospital."

Gasps and concerned murmurs filled the room instantly.

"But before anyone panics," Love jumped in quickly, "we're both okay. The baby is okay, God covered us."

Everyone let out a sigh of relief, but their eyes were still full of concern.

"It was a scary moment," Troy admitted, "but it reminded us how fragile this journey is... and how faithful God has been every step of the way."

"And," Love added with a nervous smile, "while they were checking to make sure everything was okay... they found something."

The room went still again.

Troy grinned. "Actually, they found *someone*."

A beat passed and then the realization hit.

"You're having twins?" Love's mother gasped, eyes wide.

Love nodded, her eyes glistening. "We're having a boy and a girl."

Cheers and shouts of joy filled the room instantly. Love was swept into her mother's arms, while Troy's brothers clapped him on the back. Love's father wiped his eyes, overwhelmed with emotion, and Troy's mother lifted her hands in praise.

"You've been blessed with a double portion," Troy's dad said with a proud smile.

"Yes, we have," Troy said quietly, glancing at Love.

They handed out new ultrasound photos, the ones of both babies. One labeled *Baby A - Jeremiah*, and the second labeled *Baby B - Isabella*.

Two tiny profiles. Two heartbeats. Two answers to prayer.

The rest of the evening was filled with joy, questions, and laughter. Both moms already started listing baby shower ideas and guessing who each baby would look like. The dads debated over who would spoil the twins more, and the siblings were already arguing over who would get to babysit first.

As the night wound down and the families began to say their goodbyes, Love looked around the living room, at the joy, the love, the shared awe, and leaned into Troy.

"I was so scared earlier this week," she whispered. "But now? I've never felt more covered."

Troy kissed her temple and smiled. "We're not walking this road alone. God is with us, and so is our village."

CHAPTER 12

As the weeks rolled on and the third trimester loomed closer, the preparations for the twins began to take full swing. The news of having not just one, but *two* babies had sent their families, and Love's Pinterest boards, into overdrive.

Though both Love and Troy were still working full-time, their daily rhythms had shifted. Troy made it a point to leave work earlier and check in with Love more often throughout the day. Love, though dedicated to her job, had scaled back her responsibilities and was under strict instructions from both her doctor *and* her husband to "take it easy." Her workdays now included longer breaks, her favorite ice pebble cup always nearby, and a cushioned footrest under her desk that Julie had sneakily ordered for her.

Julie had become her office guardian angel, keeping her hydrated, calm, and hidden from any unnecessary stress. "Queen status until the babies arrive," she'd joke, bringing her snacks and organizing her inbox.

Back at home, baby prep was in full bloom. The nursery was slowly transforming into a soft wonderland of pastels, books, and fluffy animals. One side of the room was dressed in soft blue with a name banner that read *Jeremiah Isaiah*, while the other side was adorned in gentle blush tones with *Isabella Abigail* stitched in elegant script. Neutral colors and gold accents tied everything together, making the space feel warm, peaceful, and perfectly balanced.

Troy took pride in assembling every crib, painting walls, and reading endless articles on twin schedules. He'd often pause mid-task to place his hand on Love's belly, feeling the growing kicks of their little ones and whispering affirmations to them.

"Daddy's got you," he'd say quietly. "And God's already ahead of you."

Love would smile, resting nearby with her feet propped up, watching the man she loved become a father before her eyes.

As March approached, the long-awaited *baby shower weekend* arrived. Their families had pulled together a beautiful celebration at a local event space that felt like an extension of home. The theme was *"Twice the Love, Double the Blessing"*, with soft ivory, dusty rose, and muted blue hues draped across the venue. Balloons framed the entrance, and little onesies on a clothesline spelled out "Team Hayes."

The tables were adorned with elegant centerpieces of fresh flowers and baby-themed cupcakes, while soft worship music played in the background. A beautiful wooden sign at the front displayed "Welcome, Jeremiah & Isabella."

Love entered, her belly round and glowing beneath her soft, blush maternity dress. Troy never left her side, beaming with pride in his crisp button-down shirt that read "Daddy x2." Her shirt read "Mama Bear (with a double heart)." Everyone stood and clapped as they walked in.

The shower was filled with games, food, laughter, and so many gifts that the table couldn't hold them all. There were twin onesies, personalized blankets, diaper cakes taller than the toddlers, and more bottles and pacifiers than they could've imagined.

At one point, Troy stood up and tapped his glass gently, asking for everyone's attention. With Love holding his hand, he said, "We just want to thank all of you. For the prayers, for the support, and for celebrating not just the arrival of our children, but the journey Love and I have walked to get here. God has truly doubled our portion—and we know we're not raising these babies alone."

Tears glistened in the eyes of their mothers, while everyone else stood and clapped again, affirming that sentiment.

As the sun set and the party winded down, Love and Troy sat together on a bench outside the venue. She leaned her head on his shoulder, exhausted but full.

"I can't believe how much love we felt today," she whispered.

"I can," he replied, kissing the top of her head. "Because you deserve every bit of it, Love. And so do our babies."

She smiled, hand resting over her belly where two little miracles stirred beneath her skin.

They didn't know exactly what the future held. Sleepless nights. Bottles. Double diapers. But what they did know, without a doubt, was that they were surrounded, supported, and sustained by grace.

CHAPTER 13

As the calendar flipped to the final few weeks of pregnancy, the anticipation in the Hayes household was electric. Every room was baby-ready, every bag was packed, and every phone call from Love had Troy on high alert.

By now, Love had officially transitioned to working from home. Her company, understanding of her condition and the unexpected turn of having twins, allowed her to wrap up her final projects remotely. Her workspace had moved from her office downtown to a cozy corner of their living room, complete with extra pillows, a heating pad, and a constant stash of her favorite snacks and ice chips nearby.

Though her belly had grown round and firm, stretching her maternity clothes to their limit, Love still showed up to virtual meetings with a soft smile and glowing skin, tired, yes, but radiant with purpose.

"Okay little ones," she would whisper to her belly before each call, "let's behave for Mama's meeting."

And as if on cue, Isabella would kick. Jeremiah would shift. And Love would sigh and shake her head with a soft chuckle.

Troy, ever watchful, popped his head in between meetings. "Need anything? Ice? A break? A foot rub?"

"Always a foot rub," she'd grin.

Evenings were sacred now. With the nursery ready, they spent their time reading parenting books, praying over the cribs, and practicing breathing techniques, though Troy had a habit of being overly dramatic with his counts, making Love burst into laughter even mid-contraction practice.

Despite the fatigue, there was sweetness in these slow, expectant days. Her mother stopped by with meals, making sure she had everything she needed. Troy's mom sent boxes of baby clothes and tiny socks with handwritten notes tucked inside. Both families checked in constantly, offering support and love from all sides.

On one quiet Saturday, Troy found her standing in the nursery, her hands gently resting on each crib rail.

"You okay?" he asked softly, wrapping his arms around her from behind.

"I'm good," she whispered. "Just trying to remember every detail. It won't be this quiet for much longer."

Troy nodded, kissing her softly. "It's a good kind of quiet. The kind that comes right before the most beautiful music."

Their hospital bags sat by the door, packed with matching swaddles, tiny going-home outfits, and a letter of prayer Love had written to be read aloud when the babies arrived.

One night after dinner, they stood in the kitchen, swaying gently to soft worship music playing from the speaker. Her belly nestled between them, the babies kicking as if dancing too.

"Are you nervous?" Love asked, resting her cheek against Troy's chest.

Troy looked down at her with warmth in his eyes. "Only about one thing."

"What's that?"

"That I might cry harder than the babies when I see them for the first time."

They both laughed, their hearts full and their faith stronger than ever. The journey hadn't been easy, adjusting to marriage, the surprise of twins, the ups and downs of pregnancy, but it had deepened their bond and sharpened their trust in God.

As the final countdown began, the message on the fridge, handwritten and underlined by Love months earlier, grew more powerful with each passing day:

"For this child we have prayed."

And now, *for these* children... they were ready.

CHAPTER 14

Love's contractions started softly at first, just a mild cramping that she could easily dismiss. But as the night wore on, they grew stronger, more intense. She woke up in a sweat, gripping the edge of the bed as another wave of pain washed over her. Her breath hitched, and the realization hit her like a wave—this was it.

Troy, sensing the shift in her energy, was awake instantly. He sat up, rubbing his eyes and blinking into the dim light of their bedroom.

"Love?" His voice was steady but full of concern.

"I think it's time," she whispered, her voice trembling slightly.

Troy sprang into action, his heart pounding. "Okay, okay, let's get ready." He rushed around the room, grabbing the hospital bag and making sure he had everything they would need. Love's breath quickened, each contraction more intense than the last. She clutched her belly, feeling the tightness, the waves of pain, and the realization that their lives were about to change forever.

Troy helped her into her robe, wrapping a soft scarf around her neck, and supported her as they made their way to the car. He spoke gently, reassuring her as he helped her into the passenger seat. "We've got this, Love. You're amazing. Just breathe, okay?"

She nodded, squeezing his hand as the car started moving toward the hospital.

The drive seemed to take forever, the streets dark and empty, but Troy's mind was full of love and prayer. He spoke to God in the quiet of the car, asking for strength and for peace for both Love and their babies. He knew this was the moment they had been preparing for, the beginning of their new adventure.

At the hospital, everything moved quickly. The nurses and doctors led them into the delivery room, where the team worked swiftly, but Troy never left Love's side. He held her hand tightly, whispering words of encouragement, wiping the sweat from her brow, and offering constant prayers as the hours dragged on.

Love's body ached, each contraction feeling like it was pulling her apart, but Troy was there, his voice the steady anchor that kept her grounded. "I'm so proud of you, baby. You're so strong. God is with us, every step of the way."

Despite the pain, Love couldn't help but feel an overwhelming sense of peace. It was as though every word Troy spoke filled her with courage, and the presence of God was unmistakable in the room.

The hours stretched on, and Love grew tired, but the thought of holding her babies kept her pushing forward. She could feel them, her little ones, each movement a reminder of how close she was to meeting them. The love she felt for them already was like nothing she had ever known.

Finally, after hours of intense labor, Love heard the cry of her baby. It was the sweetest sound she had ever heard, filling the room with joy. Her heart swelled as the nurse placed their baby on her chest.

Troy bent down, his eyes shining with tears as he kissed her forehead. "You did it, baby," he whispered, his voice thick with emotion.

Love, exhausted but elated, looked down at the tiny miracle in her arms. She kissed the baby's soft forehead, her heart overflowing with love. "Thank You, God, for this perfect blessing," she whispered, her tears mingling with the baby's cries.

Troy looked at Love, his eyes filled with admiration and awe. "I love you," he said softly, kissing her cheek as they both looked down at the precious little one they had brought into the world together.

In that moment, time seemed to stand still. Their hearts beat as one, a family now, bound together in a way they had never imagined. With their baby in their arms, their love had deepened, and their faith had been strengthened. They had made it through this journey together, and this was only the beginning of the beautiful life ahead.

And in the quiet of the room, as they held their child, they both whispered a prayer of gratitude and joy for the incredible miracle that had just begun.

CHAPTER 15

Bringing their babies home was a surreal experience, one that Love and Troy had imagined for months but could never have fully understood until they were holding their little ones in their arms. The house, which had once seemed so quiet and full of promise, now felt alive with the sounds of gentle coos, soft cries, and the constant rustling of diapers being changed. Every corner of their home had been touched by the joy of their babies—from the nursery filled with pastel blankets and soft toys to the cozy living room where they'd spend their nights rocking the babies to sleep. The air, once still and calm, now vibrated with the sweet chaos of parenthood.

The sleepless nights stretched on endlessly. Love and Troy often took turns getting up to soothe their newborns, their bodies aching from the lack of rest, but their hearts full of love. Every time they looked at their babies, it was a reminder that this was what they had prayed for—a precious life that they would nurture and love for the rest of their days. The exhaustion was real, but the joy was immeasurable.

Though it was overwhelming at times, they weren't alone in this new chapter. Their families, understanding the monumental shift that came with having two babies, were there every step of the way. Love's mom, always a source of wisdom and comfort, came over almost every day, eager to help with everything from preparing meals to simply holding a baby while Love and Troy took a much-needed nap. Her warm presence was a soothing balm in the whirlwind of new parenthood.

Troy's siblings also rallied around them. His younger sister, Grace, moved in for a few days to help with the daily tasks that piled up, laundry, washing bottles, and even playing the role of "nanny" when Love and Troy needed a moment to themselves. Grace's laughter filled the house as she rocked the babies and chatted with them like they could understand every word. It made Love smile to see how supportive their families were, their presence a reminder of the strong foundation of love and support surrounding their little family.

One evening, after a particularly rough night of interrupted sleep, Love found herself sitting in the living room, nursing one of the babies in the quiet. Troy, exhausted but still attentive, sat beside her, rubbing her back and offering quiet words of encouragement. "You're doing amazing, baby," he whispered, watching her with eyes full of admiration.

As they sat there, Love's mother arrived with a big pot of homemade chicken soup and a tray of freshly baked cookies. She had been so excited to help in any way she could, and Love couldn't help but feel incredibly grateful for her support. "I thought you might need a little pick-me-up," her mom said with a smile as she set the food on the table.

Troy was quick to jump in, giving her a grateful smile. "You're a lifesaver, Mom," he said, his exhaustion evident but his gratitude clear.

Their parents weren't the only ones offering help. Love's sisters, cousins, and aunts made regular trips to their home, offering to stay for a few hours to let Love and Troy sleep or run errands. They took turns helping with the babies, cleaning the house, and organizing the ever-growing collection of baby clothes. They each left a little piece of themselves behind with every visit—a meal, a hug, or a word of encouragement that helped sustain Love and Troy through the more challenging moments.

Despite the chaos, there was a profound sense of peace that came with the love and support that surrounded them. Love often found herself watching Troy interact with their babies—his gentle touch, his soft whispers, and the way he seemed to pour all of his love into every movement. There were moments when she caught herself just staring at him, heart full of love for the man who had stood by her side through every high and low. He wasn't just her partner; he was the father of their children, the person who would always have her back, and together, they were creating something beautiful.

As the days passed, Love gradually settled into a rhythm, thanks to the support of their families. She was learning to trust in herself and in the process, even on the sleepless nights when everything felt overwhelming. Every now and then, they would steal a quiet moment together, holding hands while the babies slept, their hearts connected in a way that only new parents could understand.

Troy, too, had moments when the weight of it all would hit him, but then he'd look at Love, and he would find his strength again. Seeing her thrive as a mother and partner was the greatest gift he could have ever asked for. They had made it through the hardest part—bringing their babies into the world—and now, they were embarking on the journey of raising them together, surrounded by family, love, and support.

Every little smile, every soft coo, every peaceful nap was a blessing. Love often found herself marveling at how far they had come, from those early days of pregnancy filled with excitement and uncertainty to this new chapter of parenthood, where their dreams had finally come true.

With their families' help and the love that enveloped them, Love and Troy knew they had the strength to face whatever came next. The road ahead wouldn't always be easy, but it would be filled with the beautiful chaos of raising two precious children. And in that chaos, they would continue to find joy, love, and an unwavering faith in God's plan for their family.

One Sunday, several weeks after they had brought their babies home, Love and Troy stood in church as a family for the first time. The soft light filtered through the stained glass windows, casting a warm glow on the congregation, who gathered around them, sharing in their joy. It was a moment of celebration, of new beginnings, of love, and of faith.

Love cradled their baby in her arms, feeling the gentle weight of their child against her chest. Her heart was full, overflowing with gratitude for this life they had created. Troy stood beside her, his arm securely around her waist, a proud smile on his face. The joy radiating from him was contagious, and as she looked up at him, Love couldn't help but feel overwhelmed by the beauty of it all. He was her rock, and seeing him so content, so happy in this moment, made her heart swell with love.

As the pastor began to pray over their children, Love's mind wandered back to all the moments that had led them here. She thought of the months of pregnancy, the excitement, the fears, the love they had poured into preparing for their children's arrival. Then there had been the labor, exhausting and painful, but the moment their babies had been placed in their arms, it had all felt worth it. Sleepless nights followed, filled with feeding, changing, and rocking their babies to sleep. Yet, in each of those moments, no matter how tired or overwhelmed they felt, Love knew they had been blessed beyond measure.

And now, here they were, standing in the church, surrounded by their loved ones, dedicating their child to God. It was a sacred moment—a promise to raise their children in faith, to guide them with love, and to always trust in God's plan for their family.

Love whispered softly to Troy, her voice thick with emotion, "No matter what comes, we'll always have each other." Her words were a promise, a vow they had made when they first met, but now they had a new depth. Together, they had faced challenges, and they would face more, but as long as they had each other, they could get through anything.

Troy looked down at her, his eyes full of warmth and love, and pressed a kiss to her forehead. "Always," he whispered, his voice thick with emotion. In that one word, they both knew that no matter what the future held, no matter the challenges or triumphs, they would always be there for each other. They would face the world together, their love and faith carrying them through it all.

As the prayer continued, Love held their baby close, feeling a quiet peace wash over her. The future was uncertain, but one thing was for sure, they had each other. With that certainty, they had everything they needed to face whatever came next. The love they shared, the family they had built, and their unwavering faith in God were the foundation upon which they would stand.

After the service, as they gathered with family and friends to celebrate the dedication, Troy's phone buzzed in his pocket. He glanced down at the screen, his brow furrowing slightly as he saw a text from an unfamiliar number. He knew that a response would have to wait, but as he excused himself for a moment, Love didn't think much of it. She continued to smile and chat with her family, her heart still full from the special moment.

Troy stepped outside into the quiet courtyard, taking a deep breath to steady himself. The celebration inside continued, but his mind was elsewhere. His phone buzzed again, he glanced at the screen and saw another text from that same unfamiliar number. He was unsure of who it was. As he started to open the text the phone began to ring.

"Hello?"

"Troy, hey there sexy" the voice on the other end was calm but familiar.

Who is this? Troy asked.

Really, don't tell me you forgot this voice, the woman responded.

He stayed silent.

This is Kim, she responded.

Kim? Kim who? Troy asked.

Kim, the woman you dated and almost married.

Troy got silent.

Hey luv you still there?

I'm here but I'm not your luv. How did you get my number?

Ummm well, I called your office and told them I was a contractor and that it was urgent so they gave me your cell.

Why would you do that? What do you want Kim?

Why do you sound so irritated, she asked?

Why are you calling me, what do you want?! He asked, very irritated.

There is something we need to discuss and it is important.

What Kim?! What do we need to talk about?

She sighed.

Troy's stomach clenched. "What's going on?" he asked, keeping his voice measured, stepping further away from the church doors to shield himself from any potential prying eyes and ears.

I need to see you and talk to you about this to your face.

Troy felt a sudden weight press down on his chest. "What do you mean?" he whispered, glancing back toward the church, half-expecting Love to come out and see him talking to his ex. He didn't want her to know about this, not now.

"I... I just need to explain everything in person. It's about some things that happened in the past. And I know you want to see me, don't act like you don't miss me, she said in a light sexy voice.

Troy hesitated, feeling a pull between wanting to protect Love from unnecessary worry and the need to understand what Kim was talking about. "I don't," he replied, after a long pause. I am happily married with a beautiful wife and I don't have time for this!

"Yeah, yeah. Troy we need to meet soon! How is tomorrow?

No, we cannot meet tomorrow. I am not leaving my wife and children to come meet you.

Children? I knew you were married but I wasn't told about your children, she said with irritation in her voice.

"Troy, I don't want to do this over the phone," Kim insisted. "It's about more than just us, Troy. I think you need to hear me out. We're both involved in this, and I don't want you blindsided."

His heart was beating faster now, but he pushed aside the rising panic. "Blindsided? By what? I'll just call you later with a time and place. I don't want to cause any issues with my family so keep this quiet."

There was a long pause on the line, and Troy felt the tension grow. "I won't tell anyone," Kim finally said.

Troy exhaled slowly, trying to gather his thoughts. "I'll reach out to you tomorrow. But remember, this stays between us."

"Of course," Kim replied. "I'll be waiting on your call."

As Troy hung up the phone, a wave of uncertainty washed over him. He stared at the screen for a moment, his mind racing. He wasn't sure what Kim wanted to talk about, but he knew he had to deal with it. He couldn't let it affect Love, not today or ever. It was supposed to be a day of joy and celebration, but now he had something else to carry, something he couldn't share with her yet.

Taking one last deep breath, he returned to the celebration, pretending everything was normal. But in the back of his mind, the conversation with Kim lingered, and he couldn't shake the feeling that his past was about to collide with his present in a way he never saw coming.

When he returned to Love's side, she looked at him with a smile, her eyes sparkling with the happiness of the day. She looked down at their babies, smiling. Troy smiled back, but the weight of the conversation still lingered in the back of his mind. He kissed Love on the cheek, squeezing her hand. "I love you," he whispered.

"I love you, too," she responded, giving him a knowing look that told him she could see something was on his mind. But, for the moment, he chose not to share. Not now. He wanted to protect the peace of the day, allowing them to savor the love and joy that filled the room.

As the day continued, filled with laughter and shared memories with family and friends, Troy pushed the worry from his mind, focusing on the present. They were together. They were happy. And nothing else mattered at that moment.

But as the night drew on, Troy knew he would have to face whatever news had come his way. He didn't want to worry Love, but he also knew that whatever the future held, they would face it together. With love, faith, and each other, they could handle whatever came next.

ABOUT THE AUTHOR

Blue Kendria Berry is a proud native of Columbia, SC, whose journey has taken her across many places, thanks to her family's deep-rooted military background. A devoted child of Yahweh, she carries a profound passion for His people and the art of storytelling.

Her professional career spans both the legal field and customer service, where her commitment to excellence has always been evident. However, her love for writing began much earlier—back in the 5th grade—when she penned her first book of short stories. Over the years, she continued crafting multiple stories and novellas, eventually writing her first novel in 2010. In 2023, she embarked on this novella, a labor of faith and inspiration, which she proudly completed in December 2024 and published in January 2025.

Beyond writing, Blue is a dynamic entrepreneur. She is the owner of **Blue's Notary Services** and **Beautiful Kreations**, a thriving skincare brand specializing in handcrafted body scrubs and body butters. Her creativity and determination shine through in every endeavor she pursues.

Above all, Blue is a devoted mother to an extraordinary daughter who has followed in her footsteps as both an author and entrepreneur, continuing a legacy of creativity and resilience. Stay tuned for more inspiring works from Blue Kendria Berry in the near future!

Find additional resources and information about
Blue Kendria Berry at
Website - www.beautifulkreations.shop
Facebook - @Blue Kendria
Tiktok - @Blue_Kendria
Instagram - @beautifulkreationsllc

www.ingramcontent.com/pod-product-compliance
Lightning Source LLC
LaVergne TN
LVHW061531070526
838199LV00027B/602/J